C000245877

For the
Lord
we
Love

Your study guide to
The Lausanne Covenant

JOHN STOTT

The Didasko Files

This growing series takes its name from the New Testament Greek verb *didasko*, meaning 'I teach'. We trust it will serve the world's Church by helping Christians to grow in their faith. The series was founded in 2007 by the International Fellowship of Evangelical Students (IFES), a global movement now in over 150 countries working to proclaim Christ in the world's universities. www.ifesworld.org

IFES plays an active role in The Lausanne Movement

Editor's note

The Lausanne Covenant, drawn up in July 1974, was published with an exposition and commentary in 1975. This exposition and commentary, while slightly abbreviated and updated, is published here much as it stood when it first appeared, with extra study questions added. References to Scripture in the Covenant echo the Revised Standard Version of the Bible.

Designed by Chris Gander

Printed in Great Britain by Bell & Bain Ltd., Glasgow

For the
Lord
we
Love

Your study guide to
The Lausanne Covenant

CONTENTS

FOREWORD

Church councils date back to the Council of Jerusalem (Acts 15). These councils have produced a rich heritage of significant documents over the centuries - confessions and creeds which have defined the theology of the Church. The International Congress on World Evangelization, from which this Covenant emerged, stands in that tradition.[1]

As this study guide goes to press, preparations continue for The Third Lausanne Congress, to be held in Cape Town, 16-25 October 2010. Shortly before one of its planning meetings, held in Buenos Aires in June 2008, I received an email from a respected Christian researcher who has been following trends in evangelical growth for over half a century. I found what he wrote compelling:

> 'Evangelicalism is at a crossroads, and October 2010 can't come soon enough! It may be the last chance evangelicals really have before the darkness deepens, and the Christian moral basis of western society is swept away.'

I believe my friend is right. As we approach this Congress, we do so with a deep humility and seriousness of heart. We are living now at a vital time in Church history and in world history. We must not let this God-appointed opportunity slip by.

So why are we urging people around the world to give time to a study of The Lausanne Covenant, which was published before many readers of this booklet were born? To view the past as irrelevant is a very recent and indeed very Western mindset. To understand our times, we must grasp how we arrived in them. Learning our history is a critical part of this. To engage with the forces behind the advance of Islam, or the disintegration of the West, we must first equip ourselves with the knowledge and wisdom of our past.

John Stott and his team worked around the clock in Lausanne to complete their task of drafting The Lausanne Covenant. They received and engaged with hundreds of comments from participants. Each section, written and crafted with clarity and conviction, is infused with a spirit of humility.

The Lausanne Covenant has been a great rallying call to the evangelical Church around the world. It defined what it means to be evangelical, that is, what it means to have Scripture as final authority in what we believe and in how we live. It is a covenant with one another as brothers and sisters in Christ, and with God himself. The covenant form was chosen deliberately, as a solemn and public declaration to the world of the relationship between our faith and our lives.

Covenants are serious matters, not to be entered into lightly. They are binding agreements, and we need to read 'the small print' carefully, and ensure we have understood all the implications before we prepare to sign. The Lausanne Covenant was drawn together with great care, balancing the right words and phrases and emphases, to reflect what the Lausanne participants believed to be the weight of Scripture.

When John Stott, chief architect of the Covenant, addressed the Congress to present it in its final form, he urged participants not to get out their pens (though it seems a few had already done so, perhaps too quickly). The better response would be to meet with the Lord in an unhurried way, and only then, if they wished to do so, to sign the Covenant.[2]

As you work through it, you may want to ask yourself whether you could sign such a statement. After each section, you will find a short commentary on that section and the Scriptures which shaped it. Take time to read the Scriptures, and to weigh them before moving on to the discussion questions. If you are studying as a group, you could add further questions from your own national or local context.

The Covenant's genius is that it came out of a gathering of 150 nations focusing on mainstream, biblical, and primary issues, while avoiding controversial secondary issues. This is how it has managed to bring all evangelicals together, and become so widely-used as a foundation for partnerships across the world. The need to link arms and work together has never been more critical if we are to see Christ's gospel made known in this generation and beyond.

We trust your study of the Covenant will help you to enter into a new

Billy Graham publicly affirmed his personal commitment to The Lausanne Covenant on the final full day of the Congress, as did the Chairman, Bishop Jack Dain.

covenant with God, and that this re-publication of the document will spur further initiatives and partnerships with fellow evangelicals, for the sake of the Lord we love.

S Douglas Birdsall
Executive Chairman, The Lausanne Movement
Boston, Massachusetts

From the Chairman of The Lausanne Theology Working Group

I have just finished reading through The Lausanne Covenant again, and, as so often before, I find myself struck by its concise comprehensiveness, its profound simplicity, its breadth and balance. As you study it alone or in a group, I hope you will share my thankfulness to God, whose Holy Spirit so evidently enabled the process that produced it, and equipped John Stott in crafting it.

It reminds us of the foundations of all our mission: the person and mission of the living God; the truth of the Bible in its revelation of God and its telling the story of the universe – past and future; the centrality of Jesus Christ, his atoning death and his universal risen lordship over creation and history. But it does not waste our time wandering in the labyrinths of theological dispute. Christians can still disagree while getting on with the task of being and bringing good news to the world.

The Lausanne Covenant was prophetic in the sense of speaking in a way that applied the Word of God to the realities of the hour. And it retains its relevance and challenge now, and indeed for generations to come (as this new study guide in itself testifies). Yet it avoided being 'prophetic' in the narrower sense in which the word is used today – of tying itself to any particular brand of so-called 'end times' scenarios, which have a noticeable tendency to pass their 'sell-by' dates and recede into the mists of history.

There is a wholesome balance of biblical truth and mission imperatives. This is one reason why it is so appropriately called a covenant, since that is precisely true of the biblical covenants themselves. Lausanne makes many ringing declarations, strong affirmative statements of what the Bible teaches, and we joyfully raise our voices in agreement. Yet it never lets us rest content with signing a mere *statement of faith*. Again and again it calls for commitments to be undertaken, for choices to be made, for promises to be kept, for sacrifice to be endured, for words to be spoken and actions to be taken. I hope that the study of The Lausanne Covenant will not only strengthen your faith and understanding, but lead to some clear lines of obedience and practical outworking in the responsibilities and opportunities the Lord has entrusted to you personally.

A well-crafted balance in the Covenant, which was to prove both controversial and seminal, was between evangelism and social responsibility. (See the deliberate pairing of sections 4 and 5.) This combination is the result of allowing our understanding of mission to be formed by the Bible as a whole.[3] For the Bible as a whole gives us the 'whole counsel of God' – that is, God's mind, will, purpose, plan and mission. The Bible as a whole shows us the passion and compassion of God's heart

- for the last and the least (socially, culturally and economically) as well as the lost (spiritually)

- for those dying of hunger, AIDS, and war, as well as those who are dying in their sin

- for the landless, homeless, family-less and stateless, as well as those who are without Christ, without God and without hope in the world

The God who commands us to disciple all nations also commands us to do justice, love mercy and walk humbly with our God.

Furthermore, Lausanne sees evangelization as a process that ought never to be separated from church nurture through discipling, pastoring, training and teaching. These things were clearly integrated in the mission and ministry of the Apostle Paul, but the second, sadly, is often neglected in the haste for church growth measured in terms of numbers of converts made or of churches planted. The tragic result is fast growth without depth, conversion that never challenges underlying worldviews, syncretism, false teachings and appalling corruption and abuse among so-called Christians. It is not surprising to find section 11, on 'Education and Leadership' in a document crafted by John Stott who only a few years earlier had pioneered what is now Langham Partnership International. The aim of Langham

Partnership is to nurture depth in the local church by providing for evangelical teaching in seminaries and quality evangelical literature for pastors.[4]

We see a final beautiful balance in The Lausanne Covenant between its confident trust in God (with strong, positive, urgent affirmation of God's ultimate goal of bringing the whole world to the knowledge and worship of the Lord Jesus Christ) and its lack of triumphalism (in what Christian mission has already accomplished), or arrogant, self-confident optimism (about what Christian mission has yet to accomplish).

As with many biblical occasions of covenant-making, there is an emphasis on humility, repentance, self-examination, and shamed acceptance of so many areas of our individual and collective failure. In signing this covenant we are willing to accept the possibility that our lives may be a 'stumbling block to evangelism', and that the Church 'betrays the gospel, or lacks a living faith in God, a genuine love for people, or scrupulous honesty in all things.' The Covenant thus pours whatever responsive commitment we may make into the strong mould of God's grace. We participate in God's mission, but we do so as sinners and failures, knowing that we need the forgiving grace of God every bit as much as those to whom we bring the good news of its reality in Christ.

May these creative combinations of confidence and humility, of human energy and trust in God, of vision and realism, of joy in the Lord's doings and grief over our human failures, of strategic thinking and the Spirit's leading, of global vision and local action, of words and works – always remain characteristic of The Lausanne Movement as they are of its Covenant.

Chris Wright
International Director, Langham Partnership International
Chairman, Lausanne Theology Working Group.

PREFACE

Preface to the first edition

A theologian who teaches in Asia wrote about the Lausanne Covenant, 'History may show this Covenant to be the most significant ecumenical confession on evangelism that the Church has ever produced.' It is a bold statement. As he says, only history will tell. In the meantime, while we await history's verdict, how did it come to be written?

A fairly short statement was produced two or three months before the 1974 Lausanne Congress and sent to a number of advisers. This document reflected the content of the main speakers' papers, which had been published in advance.[5] It was revised in the light of the advisers' comments, and further revised at Lausanne by the drafting committee. In the middle of the Congress, all participants were invited to send in contributions, as individuals or as groups, and many hundreds were received, translated into English, sorted and studied. Some of the proposed amendments cancelled each other out, but the drafting committee incorporated all they could, while ensuring that the final document was a recognizable revision of what had been submitted to participants. It may truly be said that The Lausanne Covenant expressed the mind and mood of The Lausanne Congress.

I would like to express deep gratitude to Hudson Armerding and Samuel Escobar, who were the other members of the Drafting Committee, and to Leighton Ford and Jim Douglas who helped us. They worked hard and conscientiously, and we were all aware of a harmony of mind and spirit which we believe was given to us by God himself.

The word 'covenant' is used in the sense of a binding contract. We chose this term rather than 'declaration' because we did not want just to declare something, but to do something – to commit ourselves to the task of world evangelization.

The sections are all packed fairly tight, and I hope this study guide will help you to unpack them, and draw out their meaning and their implications. I should say this is a personal interpretation, and does not carry the authority of the Planning Committee. But I tried to set it in the context of the Congress papers, addresses and discussions, and to let the Covenant speak for itself. The value of the Covenant rests only in its ability to elucidate Scripture, and you will find appropriate references in the text.

Bishop Jack Dain, Chairman of the Congress, referred to Lausanne as 'a process, not just an event'. One important aspect of the continuing process will be the study of the Covenant, personally and in groups. We have included questions at the end of each section to help you.

John Stott

John Stott

Introduction to the Covenant

The Introduction sets the context, describing the participants, the mood of the Congress, and how the Covenant came into being.

> *We, members of the Church of Jesus Christ, from more than 150 nations, participants in the International Congress on World Evangelization at Lausanne, praise God for his great salvation and rejoice in the fellowship he has given us with himself and with each other. We are deeply stirred by what God is doing in our day, moved to penitence by our failures, and challenged by the unfinished task of evangelization. We believe the gospel is God's good news for the whole world, and we are determined, by his grace, to obey Christ's commission to proclaim it to all mankind and to make disciples of every nation. We desire, therefore, to affirm our faith and our resolve, and to make public our covenant.*

Setting the context

Participants came from more than 150 nations, prompting *TIME* magazine's reference to 'a formidable forum, possibly the widest-ranging meeting of Christians ever held'. On the wall behind the platform hung a banner with the congress title in six official languages: 'Let the Earth Hear His Voice'. It was a special joy that half of all there, including the Planning Committee, were from the developing world. One major sorrow was that a few countries, including the USSR and mainland China, were unrepresented. We were conscious of a deep and wonderful unity as Christians who take both Christ and his Church seriously. We praised God for his great salvation, and we rejoiced in the fellowship he has given us with himself and with each other.

It is always difficult to express a mood in words. Yet 'the spirit of Lausanne' was almost tangible. We have tried to capture it in the choice of phrases. Several speakers voiced the hope that the Congress would be marked more by penitence than by triumphalism. Self-confidence and self congratulation are never appropriate in God's children. The spirit of Lausanne was a spirit of humility and a spirit of

FOR THE LORD WE LOVE

penitence. When we sense past failures and God's present action, this leads to a look forward with hope.

This was the setting of our public 'covenant'. Does believing the gospel as God's good news for the whole world speak the language of conquest or sound presumptuous? If it does, we are content to bear the criticism, for we are ambassadors for Jesus Christ, and the empire we seek is the kingdom of God (Matthew 6:33). The risen Lord commanded us to proclaim the gospel to all mankind and to make disciples of every nation (Mark 16:15; Matthew 28:19).

1 THE PURPOSE OF GOD

We affirm our belief in the one eternal God, Creator and Lord of the world, Father, Son and Holy Spirit, who governs all things according to the purpose of his will. He has been calling out from the world a people for himself, and sending his people back into the world to be his servants and his witnesses, for the extension of his kingdom, the building up of Christ's body, and the glory of his name. We confess with shame that we have often denied our calling and failed in our mission, by becoming conformed to the world or by withdrawing from it. Yet we rejoice that, even when borne by earthen vessels, the gospel is still a precious treasure. To the task of making that treasure known in the power of the Holy Spirit we desire to dedicate ourselves anew.

Isaiah 40:28; Matthew 28:19; Ephesians 1:11; Acts 15:14; John 17:6, 18; Ephesians 4:12; 1 Corinthians 5:10; Romans 12:2; 2 Corinthians 4:7

The Covenant opens with a section about God because God is the beginning of all things. We need to encourage one another to 'think theologically', that is to relate all our thinking to God who is behind everything. We cannot talk about mission or evangelism without first talking about God, for making him

We need to encourage one another to 'think theologically'

12

known is part of his eternal purpose. He entrusts his gospel to us, and gives us his power, which works through our human weakness.

The being of God

As we affirm our belief in God, we focus on the essentials of our faith. Let's consider these in pairs as follows:

First, God is both eternal and active in time. He exists outside time and before time began (Psalm 90:2). But the God who is 'transcendent' beyond the universe is also 'immanent' within it. He created it and rules all he has made. The two truths of his being 'Creator' and 'Lord' are brought together in Isaiah 40:28, 'The LORD is the everlasting God, the Creator of the ends of the earth'.

Secondly, God is both one and three. The Christian affirms this as strongly as any Jew or Muslim (Deuteronomy 6:4; Isaiah 45:5). The unity of the Godhead is the foundation of all evangelism. It is because 'there is one God' that he demands and deserves total allegiance (Deuteronomy 6:4 5; Mark 12:29, 30; I Timothy 2:5). Yet this one God revealed himself in three stages (as the God of Israel, as the incarnate Lord, then as the Holy Spirit) to show he exists eternally in these three personal forms. So the risen Jesus commanded us to baptize converts 'in the name (note the singular) of the Father and of the Son and of the Holy Spirit' (Matthew 28:19).

Thirdly, God rules both nature and history. The apostles knew this and believed even their persecutors to be under the control of God. Notice how when forbidden to preach under threat of severe penalty, they cried to God as 'sovereign Lord'. Opposition must be part of his plan (Acts 4:28) because God 'accomplishes all things according to the counsel of his will' (Ephesians 1:11).

The purpose of God

Now we turn to his redeeming purpose. This began with Abraham (Genesis 12:1-3) and continued with Israel (Exodus 19:3-6). It finds completion (through the evangelism of the Church) in including

Gentile believers (Acts 15:14). God's promise to Abraham will eventually be fulfilled as people from every tribe, nation and language gather before God's throne (Revelation 7:9). The New Testament teaches that we are a 'people for God's possession' (eg 1 Peter 2:9). Worship of God is our first calling.

The Covenant focuses here on the relation of the Church to the world; of Christian people to non-Christian people or to secular society. It brings together two aspects: we are called out, then sent out. Jesus referred to this double role of the Church in John 17. He began by describing his own as those God had given him (verses 6,9). But those who had been taken 'out of' the world are still in it (v 11). It was not enough for them to reside 'in' the world; he had to send them 'into' the world (v18). These prepositions 'out of,' 'in' and 'into' are the key to understanding how the Christian relates to the unbelieving world.

What is the Church's mission as 'sent *into* the world'? Evangelism yes, but not that alone. Jesus came not only to witness (John 18:37), but to serve (Mark 10:45) and we must also do both. These two aspects of the Church's mission are opened up in sections 4 and 5. In summary the aims of that mission are:

to extend his kingdom Jesus talked much about this eg Matthew 6:10,33; 13:31,32

to build up Christ's body See Paul's emphasis on this in eg Ephesians 4:11-16

to glorify his name This is the ultimate aim of mission, and what we are all created for eg Psalm 115:1; Ephesians 1:6,12,14

We often go to one of two extremes. Either we are so keen to live in the world that we imbibe non-Christian ideas and standards, and become conformed (Romans 12:1,2); or we are so keen not to lose our distinctive identity that we withdraw (John 17:15; 1 Corinthians 5: 10). The best way to avoid these two mistakes is to engage in mission. We are sent into the world as Christ's representatives, so we can neither conform to it (or we cease to represent him) or withdraw from it (or we have no one to represent him to).

The power of God

We are frail, weak and fragile – but we carry a precious treasure, the gospel, and through our weakness the power of God is shown most clearly (2 Corinthians 4:7; 1 Corinthians 2:3-5; 2 Corinthians 12:9,10).

The first section of the Covenant ends with a reference (expanded in the final section) to the power of the Holy Spirit for the evangelistic task, the task to which we are invited to re-dedicate ourselves.

Questions

1 How does knowledge of the character of God help us in evangelism? Think of three or four commonly-raised objections to the Christian faith, and how we can form answers to them, based on what we know of God's character.

2 Read John 17:9-19 and summarize Christ's teaching on how we relate to the world.

3 Would the attitude of your local church to the culture around it be best described as 'conformity', 'withdrawal' or 'mission'? Give some examples. What steps could be taken to help church members to address what you may find to be wrong?

4 In one simple sentence, what is 'the purpose' of God as you understand it? On which Scriptures do you base this?

5 Identify key phrases in this section which state God's purpose, and those which state God's process of accomplishing it.

6 We are his servants and witnesses; how do our service and witness relate to our primary call to worship God?

2 THE AUTHORITY AND POWER OF THE BIBLE

We affirm the divine inspiration, truthfulness and authority of both Old and New Testament Scriptures in their entirety as the only written word of God, without error in all that it affirms, and the only infallible rule of faith and practice. We also affirm the power of God's word to accomplish his purpose of salvation. The message of the Bible is addressed to all men and women. For God's revelation in Christ and in Scripture is unchangeable. Through it the Holy Spirit still speaks today. He illumines the minds of God's people in every culture to perceive its truth freshly through their own eyes, and thus discloses to the whole Church ever more of the many-coloured wisdom of God.

2 Timothy 3:16; 2 Peter 1:21; John 10:35; Isaiah 55:11; 1 Corinthians 1:21; Romans 1:16, Matthew 5:17,18; Jude 3; Ephesians 1:17,18; 3:10,18

It may seem strange for a covenant on world evangelization to give such prominence to biblical authority.[6] Let's think about the connection. Both evangelism and the nurture of new Christians involve teaching and so raise the question 'What shall we teach?' Our content must be rich, biblical content. To distil this content we concentrate on three features of the Bible — its authority, its power and its interpretation.

The authority of the Bible

Scripture is 'the Word of God' (Hebrews 1:1,2; 1 Thessalonians 2:13); it is his 'written Word' for he caused it to be recorded to teach later generations (Romans 15:4; 1 Corinthians 10:6,11; 1 Timothy 3:14,15); and it is his 'only' written Word, for we cannot accept the scriptures of other religions (eg the Koran or the Book of Mormon) as having come out of the mind and mouth of God. Let's look at three critical words - inspiration, truthfulness and authority.

(a) *Inspiration* This does not mean that God breathed into words which had been written, or into the writers who wrote them, but rather that the words themselves were 'God-breathed' (2 Timothy 3:16, literally). Of course, they were also the words of those who spoke and wrote freely. Yet these people were 'moved by the Holy Spirit' (2 Peter 1:21) to such an extent that it could be said of their words: 'the mouth of the Lord has spoken it' (Isaiah 40:5).

(b) *Truthfulness* Since Scripture is God's Word written, it is true (Numbers 23:19). As Jesus himself said in prayer to the Father, 'Thy word is truth' (John 17:17). And since it is true, it is without error in all that it affirms. Not everything contained in Scripture is affirmed by Scripture. Let's take an extreme example: Psalm 14:1 contains the statement 'there is no God.' This statement is false, but Scripture is not affirming it. What Scripture affirms in that verse is not atheism, but the folly of atheism, 'The fool says in his heart, "There is no God"'. It is important in all our Bible study to consider the intention of the author, and what is actually being asserted.

(c) *Authority* Note the order of the three words. The divine inspiration of Scripture secures its truthfulness, and because Scripture is truth from God it has authority. Different churches may have their own creeds, confessions and traditions to govern what they teach and practise, but Scripture is the only infallible rule, and this derives from its authority and inspiration. Jesus himself made it plain that church traditions must always be subservient to Scripture, because they are human words, while Scripture is God's Word (Mark 7:1-13). Indeed, Jesus' own submission to the Old Testament Scriptures, and his provision for the New Testament Scriptures by appointing the apostles, give us one of the main reasons for accepting the authority of Scripture. The disciple is not above his master.

The power of the Bible

As we all know, our human words can be feeble and mean nothing, but when God speaks, he acts. His Word always accomplishes his purpose (Isaiah 55:11). It is powerful. Indeed it was by his Word that he created the world (Genesis 1:9ff; Psalm 33:6,9).

What is true of creation is equally true of salvation. The gospel itself is 'the power of God for salvation to everyone who has faith' (Romans 1:16). We cannot save ourselves by our own wisdom. Instead, it pleases God 'through the folly of what we preach to save those who believe' (1 Corinthians 1:21). Not that we should separate the power of God's Word from the power of God's Spirit. The Spirit uses the Word, and speaks and acts through it (eg 1 Corinthians 2:1-5; 1 Thessalonians 1:5; 1 Peter 1:12). Scripture is rich in metaphors for the power of the Word in the hand of the Spirit (eg Jeremiah 23:29 'fire' and 'hammer'; Ephesians 6:17 and Hebrews 4:12 'sword'; 1 Peter 1:23 and James 1:21 'seed', etc). Let those of us who handle Scripture in preaching, teaching or in personal evangelism, take heart and continue to do so faithfully and with humility.

The interpretation of the Bible

The last four sentences of the section touch on a paradox. Let me open this out: The message of the Bible is the same for everyone in all places at all times. God's revelation in Christ and in Scripture is unchangeable; it 'cannot be broken' (John 10:35, compare Mathew 5:17,18). It has been delivered to us 'once for all' unalterably (Jude 3). And being God's truth it possesses a unique universality; it has a message for everybody everywhere. But it does not have a dead, wooden, colourless uniformity. As the Holy Spirit used the personality and culture of writers to convey something fresh and appropriate, he illumines the thinking of God's people in every culture to perceive its truth freshly. It is he who opens the eyes of our hearts (Ephesians 1:17,18), and these eyes and hearts belong to young and old, Latin and Anglo-Saxon, African, Asian and American, male and female, poetic and prosaic. The Holy Spirit uses this 'magnificent and intricate mosaic of mankind[7]' to disclose from Scripture ever more of the many-coloured wisdom of God (a literal translation of Ephesians 3:10). So the whole Church is needed to receive God's whole revelation in all its beauty and richness (see Ephesians 3:18 'with all the saints'). Each culture and nation must share the gifts which have been given to our

national church. To encourage such sharing has been a trademark of
The Lausanne Movement.

Questions

1 The Covenant carries strong statements on the inspiration and
authority of the Bible. How do they relate to evangelism? What
difference would it make to our evangelism if we really believe God's
Word has power?

2 The Covenant draws a distinction between the Holy Spirit's work in
'revelation' (the writing of the Bible) and in 'illumination' (helping us
as we read the Bible). Why is this distinction important?

3 Think of friends, neighbours, family who do not believe in Christ. Have
they ever read the gospel narrative? Would they be willing to, if invited?

③ THE UNIQUENESS AND UNIVERSALITY OF CHRIST

*We affirm that there is only one Saviour and only one gospel,
although there is a wide diversity of evangelistic approaches. We
recognize that everyone has some knowledge of God through his
general revelation in nature. But we deny that this can save, for
people suppress the truth by their unrighteousness. We also reject
as anathema to Christ and the gospel every kind of syncretism
and dialogue which implies that Christ speaks equally through all
religions and ideologies. Jesus Christ, being himself the only God-
Man, who gave himself as the only ransom for sinners, is the only
mediator between God and people. There is no other name by
which we must be saved. All men and women are perishing
because of sin, but God loves everyone, not wishing that any
should perish but that all should repent. Yet those who reject
Christ deny themselves the joy of salvation and condemn
themselves to eternal separation from God. To proclaim Jesus as
'the Saviour of the world' is not to affirm that all people are*

either automatically or ultimately saved, still less to affirm that all religions offer salvation in Christ. Rather, it is to proclaim God's love for a world of sinners and to invite everyone to respond to him as Saviour and Lord in the wholehearted personal commitment of repentance and faith. Jesus Christ has been exalted above every other name; we long for the day when every knee shall bow to him and every tongue shall confess him Lord.[8]

Galatians 1:6-9; Romans 1:18-32; I Timothy 2:5,6; Acts 4:12; John 3:16-19; 2 Peter 3:9; 2 Thessalonians 1:7-9; John 4:42; Matthew 11:28; Ephesians 1:20,21; Philippians 2:9-11

Here we open with the affirmation that there is only one Saviour and only one gospel. Some argue that the New Testament itself contains contradictory gospels. Strange! They cannot have grasped the unity of the apostolic message (1 Corinthians 15:11; NB, the pronouns 'I,' 'they,' 'we' and 'you'), or felt the force of Paul's references to anybody (including even himself, and even an angel from heaven) who 'should preach... a gospel contrary to that which we preached to you...contrary to that which you received' (Galatians 1:6-9).[9]

What, then, about those who have not heard the gospel? Are we to say that they know nothing of God? Do we say the same of those who follow other religions? No. We recognize that everyone has some knowledge of God. This universal (though partial) knowledge is due to God's self-revelation: what theologians call either his 'general' revelation because it is made to everyone, or his 'natural' revelation because it is made in nature, both externally in the universe (Romans 1:19-21) and internally in the human conscience (Romans 1:32; 2:14,15). Such knowledge of God is not saving knowledge. This is partly because it is a revelation of God's power, deity and holiness (Romans 1:20,32) but not of his love for sinners or of his plan of salvation; and partly because human beings do not live up to the knowledge they have (Romans 1:18), and their rejection of the truth leads to idolatry, to immorality and to the judgment of God (Romans 1:21-32). So, far from saving them, their knowledge actually condemns them. And they are without excuse (Romans 1:20). So it is wrong to suppose we can be saved through other systems, or that Christ speaks equally through all religions and ideologies.

We firmly deny every kind of syncretism. It is not worthy of Christ and the gospel. Christ and his gospel are unique, and non-Christian religions know nothing of them.

The uniqueness of Christ: he is the only Saviour

We go on to define and defend the opening statement that 'there is only one Saviour'. It relies first on 1 Timothy 2:5,6: 'there is one mediator between God and men, the Man Christ Jesus, who gave himself as a ransom for all.' Notice the three nouns applied in these verses to Jesus - 'mediator,' 'Man' and 'ransom.' 'Man' alludes to his birth of a human mother and 'ransom' to his death on the cross bearing the penalty we deserved. Or, theologically speaking, these two words refer to his incarnation and his atonement. Both are unique. Neither has any parallel in other religions. And it is precisely because Jesus Christ is the only God-Man *and* the only ransom for sinners that he is the only mediator between God and us. The Apostle Peter was in complete agreement: 'There is salvation in no one else, for there is no other name under heaven given by which we must be saved' (Acts 4:12).

A rescue from the guilt of sin and from the judgment of God is urgently needed. 'Perishing' is a terrible word, but Jesus himself used it (eg Matthew 18:14; Luke 13:3,5; John 3:15,16) and so did the apostles (eg 1 Corinthians 1:18); we must not shy away from it. Everyone shares this plight unless we are saved by Christ. Yet there is something else we know, and that is that God loves everyone. And because of his great love, he is forbearing and patient, not wishing that any should perish, but that all should repent (2 Peter 3:9). Although this is the wish of God (for he says, 'I have no pleasure in the death of any one,' Ezekiel 18:32), we know that some will refuse to repent and believe, will instead reject Christ, and condemn themselves to eternal separation from God (2 Thessalonians 1:7-9). The prospect is almost too dreadful to contemplate; we should be able to speak of it only with tears.

we should be able to speak of it only with tears

Some may ask how these sentences relate to the doctrine of election (which Scripture teaches), and how divine sovereignty in salvation can be reconciled with human responsibility. Theologians have wrestled with this matter for centuries. The Bible teaches both truths. However paradoxical it may sound, those who are saved must ascribe all the credit to God, while those who are lost must accept all the blame themselves.

The universality of Christ: he is the Saviour of the world

We move from the uniqueness of Christ to the universality of Christ. These truths cannot be separated. It is because Jesus Christ is the only Saviour that we must bring his gospel to the whole world. We read that many Samaritans called him 'the Saviour of the world' (John 4:42), and John wrote that 'the Father has sent his Son as the Saviour of the world' (1 John 4:14). But let's be clear on what we mean by this great and glorious title.

We do not mean that everyone is automatically saved (for we must believe in the Lord Jesus to be saved (Acts 16:31); nor that everyone is ultimately saved (for some will reject Christ and be lost). Still less do we mean that all religions offer salvation in Christ, because plainly they do not. Other religions, if they teach salvation at all, offer it only as a reward for merit accumulated by good works; the Christian message is 'the gospel of the *grace* of God' (Acts 20:24), mercy to sinners who deserve nothing except judgment.

To proclaim Jesus Christ as 'the Saviour of the world' is to proclaim God's love, a love so great that he gave his only Son to die on the cross (John 3:16; Romans 5:8; 1 John 4:9,10). It is also to invite everyone without distinction to respond to him. The Apostle Paul understood and felt his burden so keenly. 'I am under obligation,' he wrote 'both to Greeks and to barbarians, both to the wise and to the foolish' (Romans 1:14).

We must not allow racial or social barriers to be raised as a reason for not preaching the gospel. In particular, the same gospel must be made known to Jews and Gentiles, or more accurately 'to the Jew first and also to the Greek' (eg Romans 1:16, 10:12). Some of our Jewish brothers were disappointed that the Covenant contained no reference to them. And with the benefit of hindsight we can now apologize. For God has by no means rejected his ancient people (Romans 11:1,2), and still purposes 'their full inclusion' (Romans 11:12 ff). So the invitation goes out to Jew and Gentile alike to respond to Christ as Saviour and Lord in wholehearted personal commitment. Paul called it 'the obedience of faith' (Romans 1:5; 16:26). This is opened out further in the next section.

God has given Jesus Christ the supreme place at his own right hand (Ephesians 1:20-23; Philippians 2:9). God's purpose in exalting Jesus was and is 'that at the name of Jesus every knee should bow... and every tongue confess that Jesus Christ is Lord' (Philippians 2:10,11). We too should long for the lordship of Jesus Christ to be acknowledged. This is surely the goal of evangelism. In the end every knee will bow to Christ, for even his enemies will 'be made a stool for his feet' (Hebrews 10:12,13; Psalm 110:1). And because our eyes have been opened to see the supremacy of Jesus Christ, we long for the day when every knee shall bow to him.

we long for the day when every knee shall bow to him

Questions

1 What makes the ancient gospel 'good news' to a world filled with pain, suffering and tragedy?

2 As followers of Jesus Christ, what compels us to take the gospel to the

whole world, when many people already have their own religion? What light does this section throw on the condition of non-Christians? Does it make us re-evaluate our priorities of time and energy? In what ways?

3 In John 17, Jesus prays for unity among his followers. How is this different from syncretism? You may like to look at the core beliefs which bind true Christians together.

4 Some people say we have no right to impose our beliefs on followers of other faiths. How does this section help you to reply? Are there implications for your church, if your town or city has a majority - or a minority - population of those of other faiths?

4 THE NATURE OF EVANGELISM

To evangelize is to spread the good news that Jesus Christ died for our sins and was raised from the dead according to the Scriptures, and that, as the reigning Lord, he now offers the forgiveness of sins and the liberating gifts of the Spirit to all who repent and believe. Our Christian presence in the world is indispensable to evangelism, and so is that kind of dialogue whose purpose is to listen sensitively in order to understand. But evangelism itself is the proclamation of the historical, biblical Christ as Saviour and Lord, with a view to persuading people to come to him personally and so be reconciled to God. In issuing the gospel invitation we have no liberty to conceal the cost of discipleship. Jesus still calls all who would follow him to deny themselves, take up their cross, and identify themselves with his new community. The results of evangelism include obedience to Christ, incorporation into his Church and responsible service in the world.

1 Corinthians 15:3,4; Acts 2:32-39; John 20:21; 1 Corinthians 1:23; 2 Corinthians 4:5; 5:11,20; Luke 14:25-33; Mark 8:34; Acts 2:40,47; Mark 10:43-45

In his opening address at The Lausanne Congress, Billy Graham expressed as his first hope that our ten days together would 'frame a biblical declaration on evangelism,' and in his final address he declared himself satisfied that it had done so. Many others shared the same hope and the same satisfaction. The fourth section begins with a definition of biblical evangelism, and goes on to describe its context, namely what must precede and follow it.

The definition of evangelism

The English word 'evangelism' is derived from a Greek term meaning literally 'to bring or to spread good news'. It is impossible to talk about evangelism without talking about the content of the good news. What is it? At its very simplest, it is Jesus. Jesus Christ himself is the essence of the gospel. If we were to transliterate Acts 8:35, we would say Philip 'evangelized to him Jesus', that is, he told him the good news of Jesus (compare Romans 1:1,3). But what is the good news of Jesus? The Covenant attempts to summarize it as expounded by the Apostle Peter in his early speeches in Acts (especially 2:22-39), and by the Apostle Paul in 1 Corinthians 15:1ff.

The *first* element is the death and resurrection of Jesus. The apostles also alluded to his birth and life, his words and works, his reign and return, but they concentrated on the good news that Jesus Christ died for our sins and was raised from the dead. His death and resurrection were to them verifiable historical events. And they were significant events, for Christ died for our sins, to bear their condemnation and secure our justification, and he was raised to prove that his sacrifice for sin had been accepted and that he had not died in vain (Romans 4:25; 1 Corinthians 15:17-19).

The *second* element concerned the witnesses to these events: the Old Testament prophets and the New Testament apostles. The apostles kept quoting from the Old Testament and emphasising 'we are witnesses of these things.' In brief, they preached the death and resurrection of Jesus Christ according to the Scriptures (1 Corinthians 15:3,4). Whatever the popular misinterpretations of Christ in our day, we must be faithful to the authentic, historical, biblical Jesus, presented in the

Scriptures of both Old and New Testaments.

Thirdly, the good news relates not only to Christ's death and resurrection, but to what he now offers. For he is exalted to God's right hand, and from that position of unique authority he promises the forgiveness of sins (taking away our guilt and drawing us into the favour and the family of God), and the liberating gift of the Spirit. The Holy Spirit is given to all who come to Christ, and the Spirit sets us free from self-centredness to live for God and for others.

Fourthly, to receive these free gifts we must repent and believe, turning from sins, lies and idols, and trusting in Jesus Christ as the only Saviour. The two belong together, for 'faith without repentance is not saving faith but presumptuous believism'.[10] Perhaps baptism should also be mentioned here, for this is where the apostles put it (eg Acts 2:38). Since it is administered 'in the name of Jesus Christ' it signifies publicly a change of heart, a penitent faith in the Lord Jesus.

> *Here is the irreducible minimum of the apostolic gospel*

Here, then, is the irreducible minimum of the apostolic gospel. We must never stray from these events and their witnesses, from the offer based upon the events, or from the conditions on which the offer depends.

The prelude to evangelism

True evangelism never takes place in a vacuum, but in a context. A situation precedes it; and consequences follow it. In referring to this, the Covenant uses the words presence, proclamation, persuasion and dialogue which all figure prominently in theological debate. In essence, evangelism is the proclamation of the historical, biblical Christ as Saviour and Lord. The only Jesus there is to proclaim is the Jesus of history, the Jesus of Scripture, who is 'our Lord and Saviour Jesus Christ' (eg 2 Peter 3:18). We cannot preach his salvation without his lordship, or his lordship without his salvation (1 Corinthians 1:23; 2 Corinthians 4:5).

How can we share Christ with people with whom we have no contact? In short, we can't. The first word of Jesus' Great Commission was not 'preach' but 'go'. The most effective evangelists are those who draw alongside. But we must do more than just draw alongside. Presence is not a substitute for proclamation (as some maintain). Dialogue is needed too. We need to talk seriously and to listen seriously; that is the essence of dialogue. The Apostle Paul is a great model for us.

The consequences of evangelism

Evangelism is not concerned only with spreading the good news, but also with people's response to what they hear. It is proclamation with a view to persuasion. Persuading figured prominently in the early Church's evangelism. Paul used the word to sum up his ministry (2 Corinthians 5:11); and in Acts, Luke describes Paul's ministry in that way (see Acts 17:1-4; 18:4; 19:8-10,26; 28:23,24). The apostles did not regard argument as incompatible with trust in the Holy Spirit; neither should we.

Persuasion must be honest and open. So the gospel invitation should not conceal the cost of discipleship. Jesus himself urged would-be followers to 'sit down first and count the cost' (Luke 14:28,31; compare Luke 14:26,27,33). And Jesus still calls his disciples to deny themselves (putting him before self), to take up their cross (following him to the place of execution, where self is crucified) and to identify themselves with his new community (Mark 8:34-38).

Conversion involves at least three new relationships – obedience to Christ, membership of a church (Acts 2:40-47), and responsible service to the world. It means nothing if it does not bring a change from self-centred living to sacrificial service (Mark 10:43-45).

Questions

1 Using this section as a starting point, summarize (from the New Testament but in your own words) what the good news is.

2 Compare the references to 'dialogue' in sections 3 and 4. What is good in dialogue and what is lacking about dialogue? Does the right type have a place in your own witness? Think of examples.

3 In what ways could you (and your church) be more faithful in facing people with the cost of discipleship?

4 How would you define the goal of evangelism? Why do we want people to hear the good news?

⑤ CHRISTIAN SOCIAL RESPONSIBILITY

We affirm that God is both the Creator and the Judge of all. We therefore should share his concern for justice and reconciliation throughout human society and for the liberation of men and women from every kind of oppression. Because men and women are made in the image of God, every person, regardless of race, religion, colour, culture, class, sex or age, has an intrinsic dignity because of which he or she should be respected and served, not exploited. Here too we express penitence both for our neglect and for having sometimes regarded evangelism and social concern as mutually exclusive. Although reconciliation with other people is not reconciliation with God, nor is social action evangelism, nor is political liberation salvation, nevertheless we affirm that evangelism and socio-political involvement are both part of our Christian duty. For both are necessary expressions of our doctrines of God and humankind, our love for our neighbour and our obedience to Jesus Christ. The message of salvation implies also a message of judgment upon every form of alienation, oppression and discrimination, and we should not be afraid to denounce evil and injustice wherever they exist. When people receive Christ they are born again into his kingdom and must seek not only to exhibit but also to spread its righteousness in the midst of an unrighteous world. The salvation we claim should be transforming us in the totality of our personal and social responsibilities. Faith without works is dead.[11]

Acts 17:26,31; Genesis 18:25; Isaiah 1:17; Psalm 45:7; Genesis 1:26,27; James 3:9; Leviticus 19:18; Luke 6:27,35; James 2:14-26; John 3:3,5; Matthew 5:20; 6:33; 2 Corinthians 3:18; James 2:20

Evangelicals historically have had an outstanding record of social action. In the last half century we have tended to divorce evangelism from social concern, and to concentrate almost exclusively on evangelism; this has led to an imbalance, even to a travesty of the gospel. We begin with a reference to two sentences, one of confession and the other of affirmation, which occur about halfway through the section.

First, we express penitence for neglecting our Christian responsibility and for polarizing evangelism and social concern. *Secondly* we affirm that evangelism and socio-political involvement are part of our Christian duty. More will be said about this phrase later.

This section goes on to outline the four main doctrines from which our social duty springs, namely the doctrines of God, humankind, salvation and the kingdom.

The doctrine of God

The section opens with an affirmation about God, for our theology must always govern our conduct. Notice how creation and judgment, the beginning and end of time, are brought together (compare Acts 17:26,31). God is not just interested in the Church but in the world. He created everyone, and everyone will have to give an account to him on the day of judgment. To grasp this is critical as we look at our task of evangelism. We as God's people should share the breadth of God's concerns. In particular, we should share his concern for justice and reconciliation, and for liberation from oppression (see Amos 1, 2); values laid down for society long before human beings demanded them. For God loves good and hates evil wherever these are found (Psalms 7:9,11; 11:4-7; 33:5). It is

our theology must always govern our conduct

written of his King in the Old Testament and applied to the Lord Jesus in the New, 'You love righteousness and hate wickedness' (Psalm 45:7; Hebrews 1:9). The same should be true of us all. 'Cease to do evil, ' God says, 'learn to do good; seek justice, correct oppression; defend the fatherless, plead for the widow' (Isaiah 1:16,17).

The doctrine of humankind

Social responsibility and evangelism express our doctrines of God and humankind. We are made in the image of God (Genesis 1:26,27) and for this reason we are unique on earth. Humans and animals all depend on God for their life, but the human being alone is godlike with such capacities as rationality, conscience, dominion and love. This divine image or *Imago Dei* gives us an intrinsic dignity or worth, which belongs to us regardless of race, religion, colour, culture, class, sex or age. Because of this dignity, every person should be respected and served, and indeed loved (Leviticus 19:18; Luke 6:27,35), not exploited. Only when we grasp this biblical doctrine shall we begin to see the evils of racism and social prejudice. They are an offence to human dignity and therefore to the God in whose image we are made. To insult anyone in these ways is to blaspheme God (James 3:9,10). The reason murder is such a terrible crime is that God made us in his own image (Genesis 9:5,6).

The doctrine of salvation

Salvation for many is a banned word, or considered embarrassing, or even meaningless. It can be equated by many with political and economic liberation. The Lausanne Covenant rejects this, for it is not biblical. It is however our duty to be involved in social action (caring for society's casualties) and in political action (concern for the structures of society itself). Both evangelistic and social involvement are necessary expressions of our doctrines of God and humankind (as we have seen), of our love for our neighbour and our obedience to Jesus Christ. We must not equate salvation with political liberation, yet the message of salvation implies judgment upon alienation, oppression and discrimination. Salvation is deliverance from evil; implicit in God's desire to save people from evil is his judgment on the evil from which he saves them. God hates evil and injustice.

The doctrine of the kingdom

Section five ends with a challenge to us as those born again into his kingdom (John 1:12,13; 3:3,5); citizens who submit to his righteous rule. We are under obligation to exhibit the righteous standards of the kingdom in our lives. Jesus taught in the Sermon on the Mount that members of his kingdom must 'hunger and thirst for righteousness' and exhibit a righteousness which exceeds the shallow, formal righteousness of the scribes and Pharisees (Matthew 5:6,20). He also said that we must 'seek first God's kingdom and his righteousness' (Matthew 6:33); that is, we must set these things before us as the supreme good to which we devote our lives. We must seek not only the spread of the kingdom, nor only to live by its standards, but to spread righteousness in our unrighteous world. How else can we be 'the salt of the earth' (Matthew 5:13)?

The last sentences of this section revert to the terminology of salvation, but we must remember that Jesus drew no distinction between salvation and the kingdom of God (eg Mark 10:23-27; compare Isaiah 52:7). Christians humbly claim to have been saved, and our salvation should be transforming us. 'Be transformed,' Paul commanded the Romans (Romans 12:2). 'We are being transformed,' he declared to the Corinthians, using the same Greek verb (2 Corinthians 3:18). This transformation should touch every part of us. If not, how can we claim to be saved? For faith without works is dead (James 2:20).

Questions

1 The Covenant relates duty to doctrine. Look at the biblical doctrine of either God or humankind, and think out what effect it should have on our social responsibilities.

2 If your local church takes its social responsibility seriously, how will this affect its programme? Are there more initiatives you could take personally to strengthen your church life in this area?

3 'We should not be afraid to denounce evil and injustice.' How can you or your church be more effective in this locally? How can you help make a mark on national policy?

4 A large group at Lausanne, concerned to develop more radical discipleship, would have preferred stronger wording, and suggested 'the attempt to drive a wedge between evangelism and social action' was 'demonic'. How would you have responded to this wording?

6 THE CHURCH AND EVANGELISM

We affirm that Christ sends his redeemed people into the world as the Father sent him, and that this calls for a similar deep and costly penetration of the world. We need to break out of our ecclesiastical ghettos and permeate non-Christian society. In the Church's mission of sacrificial service, evangelism is primary. World evangelization requires the whole Church to take the whole gospel to the whole world. The Church is at the very centre of God's cosmic purpose and is his appointed means of spreading the gospel. But a church which preaches the cross must itself be marked by the cross. It becomes a stumbling block to evangelism when it betrays the gospel or lacks a living faith in God, a genuine love for people, or scrupulous honesty in all things including promotion and finance. The Church is the community of God's people rather than an institution, and must not be identified with any particular culture, social or political system, or human ideology.

John 17:18; 20:21; Matthew 28:19,20; Acts 1:8; 20:27; Ephesians 1:9,10; 3:9-11; Galatians 6:14,17; 2 Corinthians 6:3,4; 2 Timothy 2:19-21; Philippians 1:27

THE LAUSANNE COVENANT

7 CO-OPERATION IN EVANGELISM

*We affirm that the Church's visible unity in truth is God's purpose.
Evangelism also summons us to unity, because our oneness
strengthens our witness, just as our disunity undermines our
gospel of reconciliation. We recognize, however, that
organizational unity may take many forms and does not
necessarily advance evangelism. Yet we who share the same
biblical faith should be closely united in fellowship, work and
witness. We confess that our testimony has sometimes been
marred by a sinful individualism and needless duplication. We
pledge ourselves to seek a deeper unity in truth, worship, holiness
and mission. We urge the development of regional and functional
co-operation for the furtherance of the Church's mission, for
strategic planning, for mutual encouragement, and for the
sharing of resources and experience.*

*John 17:21,23; Ephesians 4:3,4; John 13:35; Philippians 1:27;
John 17:11-23*

The opening section refers to God's purpose for the Church, and now
we open this up and look at the Church's mission, integrity and unity.

The mission of the Church

The opening section recognizes that Christ's mission is a model for the
Church's mission (note the 'as - so' in both texts, and 'this calls for a
similar deep and costly penetration of the world.') The Son of God
penetrated deep into our humanity and became vulnerable to
temptation and suffering. Ralph Winter introduced us at Lausanne to
the distinction he draws between three kinds of evangelism:

E-1 (within our own culture and language)
E-2 (reaching people of a similar culture and language)
E-3 (cross-cultural evangelism)

33

We must identify with those we seek to reach, striving to enter their thought world. But E-3 evangelism is likely to be the most costly because the gulf is deeper and wider.

'Sacrificial service' includes evangelistic and social action, so normally the local church will not have to choose between them. But if a choice has to be made, then evangelism is primary. Unless the whole Church is mobilized, the whole world will not be reached, for it is God's appointed means of spreading the gospel. We have a huge task which calls for focused strategy. God's purpose and the world's need both bring to the Church an insistent call to evangelize.

The integrity of the Church

Halfway through section six comes a significant 'but'. It introduces the uncomfortable question of the Church's credibility. The Church may evangelize, but will the world hear and heed its message? Not unless the Church retains its own integrity. To be heard, we must practise what we preach. Our behaviour must be 'worthy of the gospel' (Philippians 1:27). And not our individual behaviour only, for the gospel is proclaimed by the Church, and the Church must demonstrate that it is a 'radically different community,' with new standards, a new view of money and property, a new attitude to secular power with a new power of its own (the Holy Spirit), and an altogether new quality of love and care.

The cross must be central to our lives and to our message. Do we preach Christ crucified (I Corinthians 1:23)? Are we as a community marked by self-denial, self-humbling, and self-giving?[12] Otherwise the very Church which is intended to be the agent of evangelism becomes a hindrance to evangelism (2 Corinthians 6:3). Four 'scandals' (the Greek word for stumbling blocks) for the Church are singled out:

betraying the gospel (distorting its content)

lacking a living faith in God (by putting our confidence elsewhere)

lacking a genuine love for people (by failure to care)

lacking honesty in all things (within the Church and outside)

We must not falsify our message, nor must we falsify our statistical reports. The Church, of all bodies, must retain integrity because we bear God's name and so put God's name at risk.

The unity of the Church

Why should we be concerned for the unity of the church? The first reason given is theological, and the second pragmatic.

Theologically, 'we affirm that the Church's visible unity in truth is God's purpose'. In one sense this unity can no more be destroyed than the unity of the Godhead (Ephesians 4:4-6). But it still needs to become a visible unity (Ephesians 4:3) and it must also be a unity in truth (Ephesians 4:13). This is the kind of unity for which Jesus prayed. It would come about only through the revelation of the Father which he had given to the apostles (John 17:11,20-23).

On a pragmatic level, 'evangelism summons us to unity'. Our message of love and peace will always ring hollow when we are not living it out ourselves (John 13:35; 17:21). Unity should be marked by truth, but has room for diversity and flexibility. Joining together local churches, or even denominations, has not in the past brought an impetus to evangelize; we need to guard against naivety that mergers in and of themselves will take us forward in this way. Mergers can be good, and combine strengths as well as saving on costs. But we must not be starry-eyed about new spiritual energy because structures have changed. This is not how the Holy Spirit works.

Evangelicals, perhaps because we are people of passion and of conviction, can be rugged individualists, and at times we appear to prefer to build our own empire than to allow our work to be absorbed in a larger endeavour for the common good. The only unity pleasing to God is unity in truth. We may disagree with one another on some secondary issues, but we must stand firm and stand together on the great fundamentals of the biblical revelation.

The section ends with a pledge and a plea, each worth attention.

A questionnaire in the Lausanne Congress asked whether participants would favour any kind of post-Congress organization. While there was strong opposition to the notion of a centralized evangelical world structure, a comparably strong desire was voiced for evangelical co-operation regionally and functionally. What is now The

The Lausanne Movement has rather beautifully been described as 'an exchange of gifts'

Lausanne Movement was formed under the leadership of people chosen by Congress participants. It seeks to implement this desire, bearing in mind the purposes of co-operation set out here. We must plan and work together, and give to one another and receive from one another whatever good gifts God has given us. The Lausanne Movement has rather beautifully been described as 'an exchange of gifts'.

Questions

1 'Penetrate' and 'permeate' are two verbs used in section 6 to describe the Church's mission. What would they mean in practice for your church?

2 The second part of section 6 is outspoken in saying what makes the Church a stumbling block to evangelism. Examine your own life and your own church's life in the light of this analysis.

3 The Church has been described as being 'at the very centre of God's cosmic purpose'. How can you encourage your fellow church members to see it in this light? How does the Apostle Paul see it in, for example, Ephesians 1:9,10,20-23; 3:10; 6:12?

4 Section 7 is about unity and co-operation. What local initiatives in your town or city would be strengthened by Christians working together?

8 CHURCHES IN EVANGELISTIC PARTNERSHIP

We rejoice that a new missionary era has dawned. The dominant role of western missions is fast disappearing. God is raising up from the younger churches a great new resource for world evangelization, and is thus demonstrating that the responsibility to evangelize belongs to the whole body of Christ. All churches should therefore be asking God and themselves what they should be doing both to reach their own area and to send missionaries to other parts of the world. A re-evaluation of our missionary responsibility and role should be continuous. Thus a growing partnership of churches will develop and the universal character of Christ's Church will be more clearly exhibited. We also thank God for agencies which labour in Bible translation, theological education, the mass media, Christian literature, evangelism, missions, church renewal and other specialist fields. They too should engage in constant self-examination to evaluate their effectiveness as part of the Church's mission.

Romans 1:8; Philippians 1:5, 4:15; Acts 13:1-3; 1 Thessalonians 1:6-8

9 THE URGENCY OF THE EVANGELISTIC TASK

More than 2,700 million people, which is more than two-thirds of all humanity [1974 figures] have yet to be evangelized.[13] We are ashamed that so many have been neglected; it is a standing rebuke to us and to the whole Church. There is now, however, in many parts of the world, an unprecedented receptivity to the Lord Jesus Christ. We are convinced that this is the time for churches and para-church agencies to pray earnestly for the salvation of the unreached and to launch new efforts to achieve world evangelization. A reduction of foreign missionaries and money in an evangelized country may sometimes be necessary to facilitate the national church's growth in self-reliance and to release resources for unevangelized areas. Missionaries should flow ever more freely from and to all continents in a spirit of humble service. The goal should be, by all available means and at the earliest possible time, that every person will have the opportunity to hear, to understand, and to receive the good news. We cannot hope to attain this goal without sacrifice. All of us are shocked by the poverty of millions and disturbed by the injustices which cause it. Those of us who live in affluent circumstances accept our duty to develop a simple lifestyle in order to contribute more generously to both relief and evangelism.

John 9:4; Matthew 9:35-38; Romans 9:1-3; 1 Corinthians 9:19-23; Mark 16:15; Isaiah 58:6,7; James 1:27; 2:1-9; Matthew 25:31-46; Acts 2:44,45; 4:34,35

These sections bring us to the heart of the Covenant

These sections bring us to the heart of the Covenant because they relate to our core purpose - world evangelization. Five groups are mentioned: churches, parachurch agencies (ie independent agencies working alongside the church) unevangelized people, cross-cultural missionaries, and the deprived, impoverished millions.[14]

Churches

For most of the past two centuries, we talked of 'sending churches' and 'receiving churches.' The sending churches were the older churches of the West (especially Europe and North America); their missions, under God, led to the birth and growth of younger churches.

Some churches planted by the apostles seem almost immediately to have become centres of evangelism or 'sending churches' (eg Romans 1:8; Philippians 1:5; 4:15; I Thessalonians 1:6-8; compare Acts 13:1-3).

Churches can't start to engage with this aspect of their calling, and then conveniently forget about it. Only when local and national churches accept their God-given vocation will we come to maturity, and begin to look like a local expression of Christ's universal Church.

Parachurch agencies

While the Church is God's 'appointed means of spreading the gospel', the Congress recognized the role of agencies. These are mostly inter-denominational, and specialist in function, enabling churches to diversify their outreach. Some for example seek to extend their church by evangelism and mission; others to deepen it by theological education and church renewal or to concentrate on a particular means of communicating the gospel like Bible translation, radio, journalism etc, or Christian literature. We thank God for their work, yet do not assume our need of them indefinitely. The Church is God's creation, essential and eternal; agencies, however, are expendable, and cannot claim the same immortality. If they outlive their usefulness because of external changes, voluntary termination is to be recommended. All agency boards should constantly and sensitively keep adjusting the ministry to meet contemporary needs.

Unevangelized people

The 'population clock', which started at the beginning of the Congress and stopped at its end, registered a world population increase of about one-and-a-half million people during those ten days. The huge proportion of the world's unevangelized is more than a cold fact; it forces us to acknowledge our failure. The words of rebuke here can be written and spoken with comparative ease. But we will not stir action in our churches until we get the unevangelized millions on our conscience, and take them to our heart, and into our prayers in deep compassion.

Then another fact is stated, not to shame us but to encourage us, namely that now in many parts of the world there is an unprecedented receptivity to the Lord Jesus Christ. There are now more Christians in more countries than ever before. We are living in times of greater opportunity for world evangelization than world history has ever known. We cannot be pessimistic. The need is for Christians with the vision, the courage and the commitment to respond to this challenge and opportunity.

Cross-cultural missionaries

The face of world mission has been transformed since the Covenant was first written. Thousands of missionaries from the Global South are serving with great effect in the West; thousands more are serving cross-culturally in their own nations or in nearby nations. While in certain situations a reduction in cross-cultural missionaries, or in outside funding, may still be worth considering, the Covenant qualifies this statement in three ways:

First, such a situation is likely to arise only in an evangelized country.

Secondly, the purpose of such a reduction would be to facilitate a deepening self-reliance. Missionaries have sometimes stayed on too long in leadership roles and impeded the development of the Church's own leaders, perpetuating immature dependence. We need to own this failure.

Thirdly, the ultimate objective would not be to reduce overall missionary advance, but to further it, for it would release resources for unevangelized areas. Our desire should be to increase the available mission force. We dare not impose any limit on the number of such workers. But there is no room for the proud and the dominant; we need servants, who hold out the word of life in love and in humility.

What, then, is our goal? It should be, by all available means and at the earliest possible time (no date is given), that every person will have the opportunity to hear, and not only to hear in some casual or superficial way, but so to hear as to understand and, by God's grace, receive the good news.

The impoverished millions

The deprived, poor and hungry are introduced in the context of evangelism. World evangelization will mean sacrifice. We may not all give an identical definition of justice and injustice, or share the same economic or political theories and remedies. But we are all appalled by the immense numbers of people who do not have enough to eat, whose shelter and clothing are inadequate, and whose opportunities for education, employment and medical care are minimal. Every Christian should be shocked by this and never become de-sensitised through the familiarity of the images we see on television or on the web (Isaiah 58:6,7).

Those of us who live in comfort have a duty to develop a simple lifestyle. Perhaps no expression in the Covenant caused more anxious thought in would-be signatories at Lausanne than this. What does it mean for the affluent to develop a simple style of living? Some wished that the adjective were a comparative and read 'a simpler lifestyle.' But even this would pose problems for us: how much simpler? And, in any case, simpler than what? 'Poverty,' 'simplicity' and 'generosity' are all relative and are bound to mean different things to different people. For example, running water, let alone constant hot water, is regarded as a wonderful luxury by those who have to queue for water at the village well, which sometimes dries up. But in other parts of the world it is a given, no matter how simply one lives.

Perhaps no expression in the Covenant caused more anxious thought than this

Scripture lays down no absolute standards. It does not encourage an austere and negative asceticism, nor does it forbid the possession of private property (Acts 5:4); and it commands us to enjoy with gratitude the good gifts of our Creator (eg I Timothy 4:1-5; 6:17). But it implies that some measure of equality is more pleasing to God than disparity, and its appeal to believers to be generous is based on the

grace of our Lord Jesus Christ, because grace means generosity
(2 Corinthians 8:8-15).

Every Christian should be content with the necessities of life

Every Christian should be content with the necessities of life (I Timothy 6:6-8), but every Christian must make his own conscientious decision before God where he draws the line between necessities and luxuries. It is certainly a sin to eat too much, and to waste food, especially when so many are starving. One way to decide whether we need something is to consider whether we use it. Perhaps we should all go through our belongings (including our clothes) annually, and give away what we do not use. The section concludes that the development of a simple life style will not only be right in itself out of a caring solidarity with the poor, but also enable us to contribute more generously to both relief and evangelism. These good works are almost everywhere hampered by a shortage of money.

Questions

I Section 8 states that all churches should be asking God and themselves what they should be doing to advance God's Kingdom. If you had the opportunity, how would you advise your church leaders in this regard?

2 If you share in, or support, a mission agency, how do you evaluate its effectiveness?

3 Section 9 sets a goal. What is it? Can you make any personal contribution to its achievement?

4 'A simple lifestyle.' What might it mean for you to develop a 'simple' or 'simpler' lifestyle? Give specific examples which you can measure in a year's time.

🔟 EVANGELISM AND CULTURE

The development of strategies for world evangelization calls for imaginative pioneering methods. Under God, the result will be the rise of churches deeply rooted in Christ and closely related to their culture. Culture must always be tested and judged by Scripture. Because men and women are God's creatures, some of their culture is rich in beauty and goodness. Because they are fallen, all of it is tainted with sin and some of it is demonic. The gospel does not presuppose the superiority of any culture to another, but evaluates all cultures according to its own criteria of truth and righteousness, and insists on moral absolutes in every culture. Missions have, all too frequently, exported with the gospel an alien culture, and churches have sometimes been in bondage to culture rather than to Scripture. Christ's evangelists must humbly seek to empty themselves of all but their personal authenticity in order to become the servants of others, and churches must seek to transform and enrich culture, all for the glory of God.

Mark 7:8,9,13; Genesis 4:21,22; 1 Corinthians 9:19-23; Philippians 2:5-7; 2 Corinthians 4:5

1️⃣1️⃣ EDUCATION AND LEADERSHIP

We confess that we have sometimes pursued church growth at the expense of church depth, and divorced evangelism from Christian nurture. We also acknowledge that some of our missions have been too slow to equip and encourage national leaders to assume their rightful responsibilities. Yet we are committed to indigenous principles, and long that every church will have national leaders who manifest a Christian style of leadership in terms not of domination but of service. We recognize that there is a great need to improve theological education, especially for church leaders. In every nation and culture there should be an effective training programme for pastors and laity in doctrine, discipleship, evangelism, nurture and service. Such training programmes should not rely on any stereotyped methodology but should be developed by creative local initiatives according to biblical standards.

Colossians 1:27,28; Acts 14:23; Titus 1:5,9; Mark 10:42-45; Ephesians 4:11,12

Sections ten and eleven handle two related subjects, culture and leadership. Both have to do with churches which come into being as the fruit of missionary labour. What should be the relation of these churches to culture? What kind of leadership should they have?

Culture

Culture is difficult to define. It may be likened to a tapestry, intricate and often beautiful, which is woven by society to express its corporate identity. The colours and patterns are the beliefs and customs, inherited from the past, enriched by contemporary art and binding the community together. Each of us has been born and bred in a particular culture, or in more than one culture. Whether we are mono-cultural or have within us more than one culture, we find it difficult to stand apart from it or them and evaluate culture Christianly. Yet if Jesus Christ is to be Lord of all, that must include our cultural heritage.

Churches must develop a double orientation, towards Christ and towards culture. Christ and culture are sometimes in conflict, so evaluation is critical, or there will be danger.

Culture (the product of human society) must always be tested and judged by Scripture (the product of divine revelation); and Jesus was emphatic that God's Word must always take precedence over human traditions (Mark 7:8,9,13). Not that all culture is bad; it is ambiguous because we are ambiguous. Human beings are both noble (made in God's image) and ignoble (fallen and sinful), and our culture faithfully reflects both aspects of this. We are created in God's image, and aspects of our culture are rich in beauty and goodness. But every part of us has been affected by the Fall, which does not mean we are incapable of anything good, beautiful or true. Jesus himself said that evil people can do good things (Matthew 7:11; compare, Luke 6:32). The beauty of art demonstrates the creativity with which we are endowed by our Creator God (Genesis 4:21,22). But all culture is touched by the Fall, and some of it is inspired by the devil and the powers of darkness.

So all culture must be tested. In matters which are morally neutral, cultures are simply different rather than superior or inferior to each other. We have no liberty to assume our way of doing things (the way we talk, dress, eat, greet people, organize our systems) is better than other people's. (Revelation 21:26, but compare v27).

The gospel evaluates all cultures. It rejects idolatry which denies the uniqueness of God, merit-systems which deny the need of grace, and oppression which denies dignity. The gospel insists on moral absolutes; human customs are relative, but God's moral law is not.

Cross-cultural missions have often imposed their own home culture as if part of the gospel. The Apostle Paul, far from imposing an alien culture on others, adapted himself to their culture (1 Corinthians 9:19-23).

If churches have been confused by importing an alien culture, they have a second problem in knowing how to relate to their own national or tribal culture. If some have been too subservient to their local culture, others have been too critical of it, and have failed to develop any music, liturgy, art, architecture, or literature in their own national idiom. But churches should go beyond reacting to the culture that is already there, and take initiatives to influence it, for God's glory.

Following the example of the Son of God who 'emptied himself' of his glory in order to serve (Philippians 2:5-7), Christ's evangelists are called to give up their home culture, and adapt to the culture of those among whom they labour; to give up cultural status, power, privileges and prejudices, indeed all but personal authenticity. This is how we can become the servants of others (2 Corinthians 4:5).

Leadership

You will see that section 11, 'Education and Leadership,' opens with a double confession. The Apostle Paul made neither of these two mistakes. His great ambition, he wrote, was not just to win converts but to 'present every man mature in Christ' (Colossian 1:28,29), and from the first missionary journey onwards he appointed local leaders as elders in every church (Acts 14:23).

(i) *Principles of leadership* First, we want to see an autonomous Church with national (as opposed to foreign) leaders. Paul instructed Titus to 'appoint elders in every town' (Titus 1:5), and presumably they were local men. National leaders are not immune from the sins of pride, power-hunger, and pomposity. So our longing is for those who draw their inspiration not from secular government but from Christ's teaching and example as one who serves (Mark 10:42-45; compare 2 Corinthians 4:5; I Peter 5:3).

(ii) *Training for leadership* The problems facing the Church are always basically theological. So the Church needs leaders who have learned to think theologically, and can apply Christian principles to every situation. Pastors need to be 'apt teachers' (I Timothy 3:2) and must also 'hold firm to the sure word as taught' so that they may be able 'to give instruction in sound doctrine, and also to confute those who contradict it' (Titus 1:9).

There was much discussion at Lausanne about the strategic need to develop evangelical seminaries, theological education by extension, research centres, regional and national theological fellowships, and to promote the exchange of theological teachers. Many initiatives such as these have been wonderfully used in nurturing leaders, ordained and lay. Clericalism (the suppression of the laity by the clergy) is not only incompatible with the biblical doctrine of the Church as the people of God, but hinders the work of the Church by denying it gifted leadership which God has provided. Yet lay leaders also need training (Ephesians 4:11,12).

Such a programme will have at least two characteristics. *First*, it will be thorough, and should include in its syllabus not only doctrine (biblical theology) but also the outworking of doctrine in discipleship, evangelism, nurture and service. *Secondly*, it will be indigenous like the leadership being trained. It should not be imposed from outside but developed by local initiatives. Nor should it rely on any stereotyped methodology since the local initiatives should be creative. When such initiatives, besides being local and creative, are also truly submissive to biblical standards, the result should be a training programme of enormous benefit to the Church.

Questions

1 What are some of the major ingredients of your local culture? Isolate those parts of it which you think should be (a) accepted, (b) judged, (c) transformed and enriched.

2 Section 10 talks about evangelists as 'servants of others' and section 11 about leadership in terms of 'service.' Discuss the relation between authority and service in a leadership role. What books would you recommend others to read on this?

3 What steps does your church take to nurture new converts?

4 'An effective training programme for laity (ie church members).' Supposing you had the responsibility to arrange one, what would it be like?

12 SPIRITUAL CONFLICT

We believe that we are engaged in constant spiritual warfare with the principalities and powers of evil, who are seeking to overthrow the Church and frustrate its task of world evangelization. We know our need to equip ourselves with God's armour and to fight this battle with the spiritual weapons of truth and prayer. For we detect the activity of our enemy, not only in false ideologies outside the Church, but also inside it in false gospels which twist Scripture and put people in the place of God. We need both watchfulness and discernment to safeguard the biblical gospel.

We acknowledge that we ourselves are not immune to worldliness of thought and action, that is, to a surrender to secularism. For example, although careful studies of church growth, both numerical and spiritual, are right and valuable, we have sometimes neglected them. At other times, desirous to ensure a response to the gospel, we have compromised our message, manipulated our hearers through pressure techniques, and become unduly preoccupied with statistics or even dishonest in our use of them. All this is worldly. The Church must be in the world; the world must not be in the Church.

Ephesians 6:12; 2 Corinthians 4:3,4; Ephesians 6:11,13-18;
2 Corinthians 10:3-5; 1 John 2:18-26; 4:1-3; Galatians 1:6-9;
2 Corinthians 2:17; 4:2; John 17:15

13 FREEDOM AND PERSECUTION

It is the God-appointed duty of every government to secure conditions of peace, justice and liberty in which the Church may obey God, serve the Lord Jesus Christ, and preach the gospel without interference. We therefore pray for the leaders of nations and call upon them to guarantee freedom of thought and conscience, and freedom to practise and propagate religion in accordance with the will of God and as set out in The Universal Declaration of Human Rights. We also express our deep concern for all who have been unjustly imprisoned, and especially for those who are suffering for their testimony to the Lord Jesus. We promise to pray and work for their freedom. At the same time we refuse to be intimidated by their fate. God helping us, we too will seek to stand against injustice and to remain faithful to the gospel, whatever the cost. We do not forget the warnings of Jesus that persecution is inevitable.

1 Timothy 2:1-4, Acts 4:19; 5:29; Colossians 3:24; Hebrews 13:1-3;
Luke 4:18; Galatians 5:11; 6:12; Matthew 5:10-12; John 15:18-21

Sections 12 and 13 introduce a sombre note, namely, that the Church must expect fierce opposition. Jesus warned us that we would encounter much hostility (eg John 15:18; 16:4), which would be stirred up by that wicked spirit he called 'the ruler of this world' (John 12:31; 14:30; 16:11). He also promised that he would build his Church on the rock and that not even the powers of Hades [death] would be able to overcome it (Matthew 16:18). The Church has an eternal destiny, and in time and eternity is secure in the Lord's sovereign hand (Acts 4:24-28).

Section 12 begins with two facts: about the battle we have to fight, and the armour we need to wear. The Church has human enemies, but behind them lurk 'spiritual hosts of wickedness' (Ephesians 6:12). We must fight them hard as they are bent on overthrowing the church and frustrating us in our task of bringing the gospel to the world (2 Corinthians 4:3,4). Yet we cannot do this in our puny human strength. This is why we need God's armour (Ephesians 6:10-17) and to fight with spiritual weapons (2 Corinthians 10:3-5), especially with the mighty weapons of truth and prayer. We need to remember Paul's conviction that 'we cannot do anything against the truth, but only for the truth' (2 Corinthians 13:8), and that Jesus himself used this weapon against Satan (Luke 22:31,32).

The section then dares to state that we are able to detect the activity of our enemy. He is invisible, but his tactics are not, and so we are 'not ignorant of his designs' (2 Corinthians 2:11). We know from Scripture what weapons he used upon the early Church, and we know from history and experience that his methods have not changed. His three chief weapons are still error, worldliness and persecution.

Error

Jesus called the devil 'a liar and the father of lies' (John 8:44). He hates the truth and is constantly seeking to deceive us into error. False ideologies are self-evidently his work. How otherwise would intelligent, educated people believe some of the nonsense taught by other religious systems and cults (I John 2:18-26; 4:1-3)? But the devil does not limit his activity to the sphere outside the Church. He is also

responsible for false teaching inside it. Paul rejected the message of
the Judaizers as a false gospel (Galatians 1:6-9), and false teachers
trouble the Church with false gospels today. How may they be
recognized?

First, they twist Scripture (compare 2 Corinthians 2:17; 4:2 and 2 Peter
3:15-16). Instead of submitting to its authority and its message, they
stand in judgment on it and distort its plain meaning to fit with their
own ideas. They have such a high level of confidence in human
abilities as virtually to put us in the place of God. A due reverence for
God, is always a mark of true religion (I Timothy 4:7; 2 Timothy 2:16;
Titus 1:1). Trying to become like God was the essence of the first sin
(Genesis 3:5) and remains the essence of all sin today.

We have a unique dignity as we are made in God's image, but we are
still creatures, and sinners dependant on his grace. A good test of every
ideology is whether it exalts God, or whether it exalts us and
dethrones him. We *need to* 'be watchful and stand firm (I Corinthians
16:13) *and to* 'test the spirits to see whether they are of God' (I John
4:1) if we are *to safeguard the biblical gospel*. Christ and his apostles
regularly warned us of false teachers (eg Matthew 7:15 ff; Acts 20:29
ff; 2 Peter 2; I John 2:18ff): we need to be constantly on our guard.

Worldliness

The devil uses moral as well as intellectual weapons. If he cannot
deceive the Church into error, he will attempt to corrupt it with sin
and worldliness. We need God's grace to keep us faithful to the biblical
gospel; yet we are not immune to Satan. 'The world' means secular or
Christ-less society, and 'worldliness' is any form of surrender to its
values and ideologies.

Not caring about whether our church is growing in size or in depth is a
sign of worldliness. Sometimes we make the opposite mistake and
become obsessed with numbers. In a desire to see a response to the
gospel, we sometimes resort to methods which Paul would almost
certainly have included in the phrase 'disgraceful underhanded ways'
(2 Corinthians 4:2) in an effort to make it more palatable. We

sometimes even publish reports which are not strictly true to try to attract funding. Wherever any of this is found, it shows that the devil has insinuated a worldly perspective into the Church, and has succeeded. The Church must be in the world; the world must not be in the Church (John 17:15).

Persecution

The devil also attacks the Church from outside, whether by physical persecution or by legislation. So section 13 boldly grasps the issue of relations between Church and state, with reference to I Timothy 2:1-4. Governments have a God-given mandate to secure peace, justice and liberty so 'we may lead a quiet and peaceable life, godly and respectful in every way' (v2). In such conditions the Church is able to obey God and serve the Lord Christ (Colossians 3:24 and Mark 12:17), and so to preach the gospel without interference (implied in 2 Timothy 2:3-4; compare Acts 4:19; 5:29).

The Church has a duty to pray for the leaders of the nations (1 Timothy 2:1, 2a), and more, as far as it can, to be the nation's conscience, and remind leaders of their God-ordained role. So we not only call upon God for our leaders, but we call upon our leaders themselves for freedom of thought and conscience, and freedom to practise and propagate religion.[15]

Having outlined the duties of Church and state, the section turns to victims of oppression and especially those who suffer for their testimony to the Lord Jesus (Revelation 1:9). We have been commanded to remember them and even to feel for them 'as though in prison with them' (Hebrews 13:3). But sympathy is not enough; we promise to pray and work for their freedom (see Luke 4:18).

Oppressors have always imagined they could use violence to crush the Church. They have never been able to, and they never will. We know our human frailty, yet, God helping us, we too will speak out with courage against injustice, and remain faithful to the gospel, whatever the cost. It may cost us nothing to say this at the moment, but we are seeing the distinct possibility of tyranny and persecution spreading into countries which at present are free. The Lord Jesus's warning (eg Matthew 5:10-12) needs to be taken seriously.

Questions

1 Read Ephesians 6:10-20. What does this teach about Christian warfare and Christian weapons?

2 'We detect the activity of our enemy.' Do you? Where does he seem to you to be most active today?

3 Some examples are given at the end of section 12 of the worldliness of the church. Does any of them fit your situation? Can you add to the list?

4 Can you think of any practical action you or your church could take (a) in appealing to national leaders, and (b) in working for the release of prisoners?

14 THE POWER OF THE HOLY SPIRIT

We believe in the power of the Holy Spirit. The Father sent his Spirit to bear witness to his Son; without his witness ours is futile. Conviction of sin, faith in Christ, new birth and Christian growth are all his work. Further, the Holy Spirit is a missionary Spirit; thus evangelism should arise spontaneously from a Spirit-filled church. A church that is not a missionary church is contradicting itself and quenching the Spirit. Worldwide evangelization will become a realistic possibility only when the Spirit renews the Church in truth and wisdom, faith, holiness, love and power. We therefore call upon all Christians to pray for such a visitation of the sovereign Spirit of God that all his fruit may appear in all his people and that all his gifts may enrich the body of Christ. Only then will the whole Church become a fit instrument in his hands, that the whole earth may hear his voice.

1 Corinthians 2:4; John 15:26;27; 16:8-11; 1 Corinthians 12:3; John 3:6-8; 2 Corinthians 3:18; John 7:37-39; 1 Thessalonians 5:19; Acts 1:8; Psalm 85:4-7; 67:1-3; Galatians 5:22,23; 1 Corinthians 12:4-31; Romans 12:3-8

15 THE RETURN OF CHRIST

We believe that Jesus Christ will return personally and visibly, in power and glory, to bring to completion his salvation and his judgment. This promise of his coming is a further spur to our evangelism, for we remember his words that the gospel must first be preached to all nations. We believe that the interim period between Christ's ascension and return is to be filled with the mission of the people of God, who have no liberty to stop before the end. We also remember his warning that false Christs and false prophets will arise as precursors of the final Antichrist. We therefore reject as a proud, self-confident dream the notion that people can ever build a utopia on earth. Our Christian confidence is that God will perfect his kingdom, and we look forward with eager anticipation to that day, and to the new heaven and earth in which righteousness will dwell and God will reign forever. Meanwhile, we re-dedicate ourselves to the service of Christ and of people in joyful submission to his authority over the whole of our lives.[16]

Mark 14:62; Hebrews 9:28; Mark 13:10; Acts 1:8-11; Matthew 28:20; Mark 13:21-23; John 2:18; 4:1-3; Luke 12:32; Revelation 21:1-5; 2 Peter 3:13; Matthew 28:18

The closing sections emphasize two neglected dimensions of evangelism:

- the only ground on which we can hope for results (the power of the Holy Spirit)

- the ultimate goal to which we look (the return of Jesus Christ).

These are great Christian doctrines about the second and third persons of the Trinity.

Both sections begin with a clear affirmation of faith. Happy is the church which is strengthened by these assurances; hopeless are the churches which lack them!

The power of the Holy Spirit

After a reminder of the power of the devil (section 12), it is a wonderful relief to turn our thoughts to the gracious and constructive power of the Holy Spirit. Again and again Scripture links the Spirit with power. For example in the Old Testament, we read 'not by might, nor by power, but by my Spirit, says the Lord of hosts' (Zechariah 4:6). In the New Testament Jesus himself spoke of the power of the Spirit for witness (Acts I :8) and the Apostle Paul wrote that, conscious of his own weakness, he relied on the 'demonstration of the Spirit and power' (I Corinthians 2:3-5; compare I Thessalonians 1:5). We must do the same.

The Holy Spirit's power is needed in the witness of the Church; and in the renewal of the Church.

(i) *The witness of the Church.* In the Upper Room, the Lord Jesus tells his disciples that the Spirit would delight above all else in glorifying the Son (John 16:14); the Holy Spirit would be the chief witness in spreading the gospel. Only after saying this did Jesus add, 'and you also are witnesses' (John 15:26,27). We need to grasp the significance of this order, and then we will clearly see that our efforts without his help are futile.

All four main stages in conversion to Christ are the work of the Holy Spirit. *First*, conviction of sin. It is the Spirit, Jesus said, who would 'convince the world of sin and of righteousness and of judgment' (John 16:8-11). *Secondly*, faith in Christ. It is the Spirit who opens the eyes of sinners to see in Jesus their Saviour and Lord, and to believe in him (I Corinthians 12:3). *Thirdly*, the new birth is a birth 'of the Spirit' (John 3:6-8). *Fourthly*, Christian growth or sanctification is his work too (2 Corinthians 3:18). The power of the Holy Spirit is central in evangelism.

The work of the Spirit arises from his nature. A Spirit-filled church becomes a mission-minded church, as we see clearly in Acts. A church preoccupied with its own affairs is a contradiction – going against its nature as an outward-looking missional community, for the Spirit longs to flow through God's people into the world like 'rivers of living water' into a desert (John 7:37-39; I Thessalonians 5:19). Only the Spirit can turn introverted churches inside out.

(ii) *The renewal of the Church* We need the Spirit to renew the Church if we are to bring the gospel to the world. There is a lot of talk about renewal; some limit this to a renewal of the Church's unity, or the Church's structures, or the Church's experience of spiritual gifts. The Covenant paints on a broader canvas, and longs for the Spirit to renew the Church in every way – in truth (as at the Reformation) and wisdom, in faith, holiness, love, and power. We need to pray for total, wholesome renewal. The Holy Spirit is a sovereign Spirit and cannot be commanded or organized, but God graciously hears our prayers.

The word 'visitation' is used here to indicate special evidences of God's presence and special activities of God's power. For example, although God is constantly present and active in his world, he is said to 'visit' the earth when he enriches it with rain and prepares it for the harvest (Psalm 65:9). So too we may say that the Holy Spirit, who lives in us can 'visit' us whenever he exercises power on our behalf. We can have confidence that when he visits the Church in power he will both bear his fruit (Galatians 5:22,23) and bestow his gifts (Romans 12:3-8, 1 Corinthians 12:4-31, Ephesians 4:11). So we pray that the Spirit will nurture his fruit in us, and that all his gifts may enrich the body of Christ, since they are gifts 'for the common good' and distributed to different believers 'as he wills' (1 Corinthians 12:7,11).

Only then, when the Holy Spirit is free to move with power, will the whole Church become a fit instrument in his hands, so that the whole earth may hear his voice (Psalm 67:1-3).

The return of Jesus Christ

Scientific secularism has eroded the historic faith of the Church that the Lord Jesus will come again. Against this background of unbelief, our faith stands out in stark contrast. While evangelical Christians, not wanting to go beyond the plain assertions of the Bible, retain a humble agnosticism about some details of the Lord's return, we do affirm at least four truths about it.

He will return *personally* for the one who is coming is 'this Jesus' whom the apostles saw ascend into heaven (Acts 1:11)

He will return *visibly*, so that 'every eye will see him' (Revelation I :7)

So differently from the first time, he will return in *power and glory*. These words are borrowed from Jesus himself (Mark 13:26)

He will return to *complete* his salvation and judgment (John 5:21-29, Hebrews 9:27,28)

His coming will be personal, visible, glorious and final

All Christians should be looking and longing for Christ to come, and should share this great confidence that his coming will be personal, visible, glorious and final.

To speak of Christ's second coming is always to stimulate action and must be a spur to evangelism. For the gospel must first be preached to all nations 'and then the end will come' (Matthew 24:14). So the period between his two comings, between Christ's ascension and return, is by his own plan to be filled with the mission of the people of God. 'Go ... and make disciples of all nations...' he said, 'and lo I am with you always, to the close of the age' (Matthew 28:19, 20; Acts 1:8-11). We have no liberty to stop doing this before his return.

What exactly is the Church's expectation or hope? Some speak in terms of the world situation getting better and better with material prosperity, international peace, social justice, political freedom and personal fulfilment, as if this were equivalent to establishing the kingdom of God. It is our duty to work for justice and freedom (as in section 5) and in God's providence and common grace we can expect some success. But Jesus gave us no expectation that everything would get steadily better. On the contrary, he warns that his coming will be preceded by the Antichrist, and that we will see false Christs and false prophets (Mark 13:21-23; I John 2:18; 4:1-3). We will never be able to build a just society on earth. Jesus always spoke of the kingdom as God's gift, not our achievement (Luke 12:32).

We should become convincing models of social and political involvement whilst here on earth, but final redemption awaits the kingdom of glory. We may differ from one another in the precise form we expect his kingdom to take, yet all of us look forward with much anticipation to 'the new heaven and earth', which are clearly promised, where God will reign forever (Revelation 21:1-5; 2 Peter 3:13).

From this glorious vision of the future we turn back to the concrete realities of the present. It is our Christian hope which inspires us to give all our energy in the work of the Lord, because we know that our labour will not be in vain (I Corinthians 15:58). So it is fitting that we come to a point of re-dedication to the service of Christ and of one another, and that we do so in a spirit of joyful submission to his authority over the whole of our lives (Matthew 28:18).

Questions

1 It is easy to talk about the power of the Holy Spirit in evangelism. But what does it mean in practice to rely on his power rather than our own?

2 The renewal of the Church is much discussed today. What is it? How will it happen?

3 Does the promise of Christ's return make any difference to your life?

4 What is the kingdom of God? How does it spread? Give specific examples of how you try to live in the light of eternity.

5 The Covenant speaks of 'joyful submission'. How can we encourage that spirit in one another?

CONCLUSION

Therefore, in the light of this our faith and our resolve, we enter into a solemn covenant with God and with each other, to pray, to plan and to work together for the evangelization of the whole world. We call upon others to join us. May God help us by his grace and for his glory to be faithful to this our covenant! Amen. Alleluia!

As you will have noticed, the Covenant consists partly of what we believe and partly of what we intend to do; or partly of faith, and partly of resolve. It is in this combined spirit that we frame, and enter into, our Covenant or binding promise – *first* to pray together, *secondly* to plan together, and *thirdly* to work together (in that order of priority) for the evangelization of the whole world, that is to say, to bring the good news within meaningful reach of the whole population of the earth. It is a colossal undertaking and will require the mobilization of all Christians, and especially the grace of God.

We pray that God will enable us to be faithful. We know our weakness, and put no confidence in ourselves. Our only hope of remaining faithful lies in his grace, and our motivation must be his glory.

Amen. Alleluia!

NOTES

1. Many regard this Covenant as the most significant missions document to be produced in the modern Protestant era. The one possible exception is perhaps William Carey's *Enquiry (into the Obligation of Christians to Use Means for the Conversion of the Heathen)* written in 1792. Carey's treatise gave birth to the modern missions movement. The Covenant has given an evangelical definition to world evangelization. It has also provided a framework for unity among Christians globally and formed the basis for many collaborative projects.

2. You can listen to John Stott's fascinating address, describing how the Covenant's final form was reached, at *www.lausanne.org/1974audio* You will find other key addresses here too. Then click through to a range of video and print archives from that historic gathering of Christian leaders from 150 nations. Enjoy!

3. The implications of this 'integral mission' were further worked out in the Consultation on the Relationship between Evangelism and Social Responsibility (CRESR) at Grand Rapids in 1982, in a document that equally deserves close study if this is an issue that troubles you. The effect of both documents, along with similar affirmations in the Manila Manifesto of 1989, has been that The Lausanne Movement understands the term 'evangelization' in its title in terms of holistic mission.

4. For more information, visit *www.langhampartnership.org*

5. All the congress papers were printed in full in the compendium *Let the Earth hear his Voice* (ed J D Douglas, Worldwide Publications 1975). Most are available on the Lausanne website.

6. The first Biblical Foundation Paper at the Congress set the stage, entitled 'Biblical Authority and Evangelism'.

7. To borrow a phrase of Dr Donald McGavran.

8. We have made two minor word changes to reflect the original meaning more lucidly. We have replaced 'derogatory' with 'anathema' (line 6) and 'repudiate' with 'deny themselves' (line 14). The doctrine of 'penal substitution' (that God in Christ took upon himself the penalty for our sins in our place) has been strongly contested in recent years. The Covenant writers affirmed it as central to God's plan of salvation. The accomplishment of the Cross not only included the central truth of Christ bearing the penalty for our sin, but also brought 'all other benefits of his passion' (Cranmer's delightful phrase in the Book of Common Prayer). For through it, Christ entered into our suffering, defeating evil, destroying death, reconciling enemies, and redeeming creation. For a full treatment of this, we encourage you to read John Stott's *The Cross of Christ* (IVP). For a briefer explanation, see James Philip's *The Glory of the Cross: The great crescendo of the gospel* (Didasko Files).

9. Professor Henri Blocher rightly emphasized at Lausanne that in the New Testament we have 'diversity without conflict', not contradictions but 'an inartificial harmony of teachings given so diversely' as to indicate its divine origin.

10. I quote the Argentinian theologian Dr René Padilla.

11. The reference to 'God and humankind' originally read 'God and Man'.

12. This helpful reference to the cross is taken from the Response to Lausanne composed by the 'radical discipleship' group which formed itself. They interpret what they mean by adding that the Church must 'identify and agonize with men, renounce status and demonic power, and give itself in selfless service of others for God.' There is much to reflect on here.

13. Now 2.72 billion, around 40% of the world's population, live in nations with 0-2% of known evangelical believers (source: Joshua Project 2008).

14. We tend to describe mission agencies (cross-cultural and same culture) and Christian development agencies etc as 'para-church' but a true ecclesiology sees them as *part of* the Church; a kind of 'specialist arm' of the Church ministering among a sector of the community or in a particular region of the world. They may better be described as 'intra-church'. The original word is retained here. Please note that while its literal meaning suggests the idea of 'alongside', its intention was not to describe the agencies' roles as anything other than a specialist mission of the Church.

15. These freedoms were set out in the Universal Declaration of Human Rights, adopted by the General Assembly of the United Nations in December, 1948, with only eight abstentions. Article 18 of that Declaration reads, 'Everyone has the right to freedom of thought, conscience and religion; this right includes freedom to change his religion or belief; and freedom, either alone or in community with others, and in public or in private, to manifest his religion or belief in teaching, practice, worship or observance.'

These freedoms are in accordance with God's will. He gave us 'governing authorities' to punish criminals and reward good citizens, not to curtail legitimate freedoms, still less to tyrannize the innocent (Romans 13:1).

16. The verb 'to bring to completion' (line 2) originally read 'to consummate'.

The Third Lausanne Congress
JOIN THE GLOBAL CONVERSATION

Cape Town 2010, the Third Lausanne Congress on World Evangelization, is a once-in-a-generation gathering of 4,000 Christian leaders from 200 nations. It will be held in collaboration with the World Evangelical Alliance (WEA). Participants will represent evangelicals from across the Church in its broadest sense, and will include leaders of mission agencies and publishing houses, as well as Christians in business, education, government, science and technology, the arts and the media.

We invite you to join with others from your church or city as virtual participants of the Congress (16-25 October 2010). You may do this through the Cape Town GlobaLink. For details go to **www.lausanne.org** We also invite you to study with us in preparation for Cape Town 2010. You will find a brief interactive study course on our website. You may register here to join The Global Conversation – to discuss and debate serious issues confronting Christians globally. We must link arms as we chart a path forward through challenges to the Christian faith barely imagined, even ten years ago.

We now live in a post-Communist world, a post-9/11 world, a clash of civilizations where other faiths are penetrating nations in new and deep ways; a world where genocide continues, and where the emerging technologies have changed everything about the way we live, and raised questions about what it means to be human.

As change gathers unprecedented speed, we need to work, study, strategize – and pray with boldness. God in Christ is reconciling the world to himself, and has entrusted to his Church this ministry of reconciliation.

Keep in touch with the theological, practical and cultural challenges in world evangelization by signing up at www.lausanne.org to receive our regular email alerts. On our website you will also discover a wealth of resources from previous congresses, and from working groups and special interest committees.

www.lausanne.org   **info@lausanne.org**

TO PURCHASE

Also in this series

An Authentic Servant: The marks of a spiritual leader
by Ajith Fernando

More Precious than Gold: Read the Bible in one or two years
(McCheyne Bible Reading Plan)

Light, Salt and the World of Business: Why we must stand against corruption by Fred Catherwood

The Grace of Giving: 10 principles of Christian giving by John Stott

The Glory of the Cross: The great crescendo of the gospel
by James Philip

Further titles in preparation

To purchase

The Didasko Files are available from Christian Bookshops and church bookstalls, or may be purchased from Amazon, Barnes & Noble and other online retailers.

For bulk discount, go to your country's distributor. Visit www.lausanne.org/didasko and click 'Purchase' for details.